BROOKLYN LOCAL

Essays on Growing Up Jewish in the 1930s and '40s

D1598316

www.PoeticaPublishing.com

BROOKLYN LOCAL

Essays on Growing Up Jewish in the 1930s and '40s

by Mordecai Rosenfeld

May, 2017

Inscribed for Director
Kamensky —
with great pleasure.

Mordecai R.

Books by the author

The Lament of the Single Practitioner

A Backhanded View of the Law—Irreverent Essays on Justice

Cover Art:
Brooklyn Map
www.jazzberryblue.com
Copyright © 2014 jazzberryblue

Copy Editor:
David King

Book Design:
Michal Mahgerefteh

Published by:
Poetica Publishing Company
www.poeticapublishing.com
P.O. Box 11014, Norfolk, VA 23517

Printed in the United States of America
ISBN 978-0-9883924-7-2

To Paula with love

Table of Contents

INTRODUCTION—LOOKING BACK

The essays collected in this book describe incidents that were part of my daily life growing up in Jewish Brooklyn in the 1930s and 1940s.

Since I am the principal character in each of these one-act mini-dramas—more Puck, I hope, than Hamlet—I thought that it would sharpen an understanding of the pieces if I were to provide a brief biography of those years.

I was born in Brooklyn in 1930 and lived with my parents until I married; they had moved to 1439 Ocean Avenue, Apt. 2 A in 1927 and never moved again. When people were surprised that they had dwelled in the very same space for half a century, my father would always give the same response: "We are not gypsies."

Both of my parents were native New Yorkers but with very different ancestral roots. My Mom, nee Lillian Katzenellenbogen, was descended from one of Vilna's great Jewish families, or so we understood. Her father, Judah Meyer Katzenellenbogen (born in Vilna in 1865; died in New York in 1920), was a distinguished scholar and publisher. He was one of the founders of the Hebrew Publishing Company (established in 1901), a leading publisher of sacred texts and prayer books, and the first to publish Jewish music and a Hebrew-English dictionary. When he passed away during Passover 1920 his obituary was the leading story in the Yiddish press, with his picture on the front page; the secular obituaries recounted his extraordinary philanthropy:

He was a member of both the New York and Brooklyn Jewish Federations and of every charitable and religious institution in New York and Brooklyn. He was noted for his philanthropic tendencies.

When others would comment on our *yichus*, Mom would reply that one of the wonders of America was that people made their own *yichus*. But she always finished that thought by recounting some of my grandfather's wonderful deeds.

My Dad's forebears came from Odessa, or someplace near there, with no record of any distinction. His father became a diamond merchant a few years after arriving in New York in the 1890s, and my father continued in that business because he considered it the Family Business. It was, sadly, a struggle his whole life; one of his characteristics was stoicism. As difficult as earning a living was, he was always the punctilio of honor. When a neighbor asked him to buy back a diamond that he had sold to her a year earlier because she had a family emergency, he paid her more than she had originally paid him, explaining that the price of diamonds had increased substantially. He was a soft-spoken, educated man, a graduate of N.Y.U., who spent many evenings quietly studying religious texts, perhaps, I used to think, searching for answers.

Although we belonged to a Conservative *shul,* the East Midwood Jewish Center, our family tilted toward the Orthodox. We were strictly kosher, both inside our home and outside, even during Passover.

My father always, and my mother sometimes, attended services on Friday evenings and Saturday mornings; my Dad did not work or travel on the Sabbath, although Mom was a trifle less rigid. Every holiday was faithfully observed.

Judaism permeated our home, but my parents and older brother, Judah, were more observant than I. In a broad characterization, they were Believers and I was not—although I had no idea what it was that I didn't believe.

My atheistic leanings were not observable because I was so dutiful: I attended services every Saturday morning at the Junior Congregation and never ate anything that was not kosher, not even a hot-dog at Ebbets Field. On Rosh Hashanah, I was the shofar blower at the Junior Congregation service because we had several at home, and I could practice and make the only annoying noise that had parental approval. That annual solo gave me a halo that was not deserved.

Aside from religion, the most controversial issue was whether I should take clarinet lessons. I was tone-deaf and argued that it would be a waste of time and money. Mom's response was that no real college would accept me if the only thing I knew was baseball. To which my rejoinder was that Moe Berg was a major leaguer who spoke thirteen languages and had a Ph.D. in physics. Mom's riposte: How do you know that he didn't also play the clarinet?

Although this Introduction and the essays themselves suggest that I was skeptical of religion, I did have one spiritual experience when growing up that was almost overpowering, and I remember it vividly. It was June 6, 1944, D-Day.

Every house of worship in the City, probably the country, possibly in the world, held a prayer service that seemed to be spontaneous.

During the war, I had a large map of the world scotch-taped to my bedroom wall, with pins of different colors demarking all advances and retreats.

And then D-Day. I can still hear General Eisenhower's messages of hope to the peoples of Europe and to our soldiers and sailors. His Midwestern calm exuded confidence.

To me, D-Day was God's last chance. The world had been in a spiraling decline since 1914—World War I, the reckless '20s, the Depression, World War II, Hitler, the collapse of France, news of the Holocaust.

I pressed my father about God's absence, and even he had to abandon that old argument about His ways being too mysterious to fathom. He had no answer, but I pressed on until Mom said that enough was enough.

As I sat in *shul* that June day, I did not feel like a supplicant beseeching God's mercy. Rather, *I* had the upper hand. I was like a teacher demanding results from an under-performing student if, indeed, He even had ability:

God this is your last chance. This invasion had better succeed.

It was the only time in my life that I felt in touch with the Almighty, and I liked my brashness, and wondered at it and marveled at it and repeated it just in case He hadn't been paying attention:

God, this invasion is your last chance.

Rabbi Halpern led the congregation in Responsive Readings and Cantor Heyman chanted familiar melodies, but I hardly heard either because I was concentrating too intensely on my own personal dialogue. Suddenly I felt an unworldly glow because I was convinced, I was positive, that I had really gotten through.

I was so overcome by my spiritual voyage that I was hardly aware that the service was over. But I *knew* that victory that day was inevitable, and I wished that I could reach General Eisenhower to tell him the good news.

One year later there was Hiroshima and Nagasaki, and my restored trust in Him was rattled. Some were proud that Jews had been so prominent in discovering and unleashing the power of the atom—Einstein himself, and J. Robert Oppenheimer, Edward Teller, John von Neumann, Leo Szilard—but I didn't know enough about either physics or theology to form an opinion. Anyway, I had promised *HaShem* that if the invasion succeeded He'd always be OK with me, and I felt that I couldn't renege.

I was glad that, a year earlier, I had promised not to intrude on God's space ever again.

I spent two more years at home, dutifully attending services, blowing the shofar on Rosh Hashanah and never eating anything non-kosher, not even a hot-dog at Ebbets Field.

Then I went away to college, on my own. Mom packed a yarmulke in with my shirts, but I didn't know if I would ever wear it.

Mordecai Rosenfeld

A GHETTO OF THE MIND

I grew up in the Midwood section of Brooklyn, on Ocean Avenue, between Avenues I and J. Until I went off to college in September 1947, I had rarely ventured beyond the neighborhood's outer perimeter, about a mile in any direction.

Nor was there any reason to stray--everything one ever needed, whether spiritual, culinary or intellectual—was right there, within an easy walk. Ferdinand Magellan and Marco Polo may have had the need to wander; but they never had the good fortune of living in the heart of Brooklyn.

Spiritually, we were members of the largest synagogue in the area, the East Midwood Jewish Center. Although it was Conservative—not Orthodox—it was God-fearing enough for me. I was usually on that sacred premise on Friday nights and Saturday mornings for services; and on Monday and Wednesday afternoons for Hebrew School. That was a lot of hours every week for a lot of years—many of them reluctant, and a few, especially in my teens, very reluctant. I surely felt no need to seek the more religious settings that existed in other parts of the City—Boro Park, Williamsburg or the Lower East Side. My own precinct had provided all the faith that I needed.

Culinary-wise, the only restaurant that I ever dined at—and it was a rare treat—was Avenue J's only kosher eatery, Polansky & Nathan's Famous Delicatessen. We practically never ate out because of the cost, but in an emergency I would be given five dollars to sup at P & N's.

There was no choice because neither of the other two dining venues on the Avenue, one Chinese and one Italian, was in full compliance with the Talmud. Some neighbors thought that they could fudge those rabbinic rules by ordering a fish dinner with vegetables— or so they claimed if spotted. But my family scoffed at such half-baked escapes.

As for P & N's gourmet quality, a sample of just one bistro did not enable me to rank it with its peers, Zagat-wise. On each rare visit I always indulged in the same fare—brisket on a seeded rye, with a knish on the side—both delicious. I doubted that Parisians with their haughty *haute cuisine* ever ate anything as tasty. My only dilemma was not whether red wine from Bordeaux or white from the Napa Valley, but whether mustard from Guldens or ketchup from Heinz. Oh the joy of eating out—Avenue J, even with just one usable restaurant, had it all.

The intellectual jewel of the neighborhood was the Brooklyn Public Library, Midwood Branch. It was located on East 12th Street, just off the Avenue, and was situated above a store, atop a steep and narrow staircase. But once you climbed that mountain you reached a plateau of pleasure…tens of thousands of books, yours for the reading

4

on the spot or the borrowing. I once asked a librarian to recommend something exciting—I was nine or ten—and she plucked *The Three Musketeers* off the shelf. I have never enjoyed a book more, even to this day.

Maybe it's because D'Artagnan and his pals were always out-dueling Cardinal Richelieu's men, a metaphor perhaps for my own imagined duels with my neighborhood's religious authorities.

Some of my peers, when early teenagers, would climb those rickety stairs to search for adult books that they could read there and then, with no questions asked. But I didn't have the courage.

We had, of course, our own small library at home, located in two small matching bookcases side-by-side in the living room. But except for a complete set of Dickens that Mom had bought using coupons from the *New York Post* and two poetry anthologies (*Best Loved Poems of the English Language* and *The Book of Humorous Verses*), the rest were mostly religious texts. Those years—the '30s and '40s— were tough ones, and my father read them diligently, searching for solace and solutions. He often focused on Maimonides's *Guide to the Perplexed*, but I could never manage more than two or three pages, not even in later years.

But the most vivid account of my insularity would be to list the places that I had never visited during those almost-eighteen years before I decamped for college. I'm not talking about never having visited the Louvre or Trafalgar Square; I'm talking about never having visited the Metropolitan Museum of Art, the Museum of Modern Art if it then existed, Carnegie Hall, the Museum of Natural History or the Empire State Building. Nor do I remember ever visiting Central Park, but that was because, as I recall, we considered Brooklyn's own Prospect Park to be just as good.

I could have visited all those Manhattan places so easily because the Brighton Local subway station on Avenue J was just a few blocks away. Then I could have been in mid-town in about forty minutes, and for only a nickel each way.

As I look back and wonder why I was so content to remain so ignorant, I can only conclude that I had inherited a ghetto complex, and no wall, not even the Great Wall of China, is higher than the ghetto of the mind.

NOT SINCE JOSHUA

The world was suddenly shrinking, what the advent of the telephone, the automobile, the airplane and the dirigible.

But Mom carried astringency to an even tighter tug when, single -handedly, she reduced six hours to three. There had been nothing quite like it, time-wise, since *Joshua* (10: 12) when the sun, on command, stood still for one entire day.

Six hours was the starting point because that was the accepted hiatus between eating meat and eating a milk product—if you opted to be kosher. It was never clear what was the theological basis for this particular gap; neither the Bible nor the Talmud mentions any particular time span. But just like the development of English Common Law, someone does it the first time, and it remains a precedent that is cited and relied on forever. So we, too, of course, accepted that six-hour fiat.

The problem was that I was a particularly skinny child, and our doctor recommended that I drink one quart of milk a day; and not just an ordinary quart of Borden's, but Walker Gordons, which was given the elevated description as "Certified". Whether that status made it purer or richer, I don't remember; but it did make it more expensive, and that was always an uncomfortable issue.

Another complication: The doctor prescribed that I drink one glass of that special liquid just before going to bed because, he insisted, that was precisely when it would do the most good.

The doctor spoke authoritatively, and the need to follow his directions was never challenged. But what was a challenge was how to arrange my day.

The only meal our family enjoyed together was supper. It began at about six, after Dad came home from his office in Manhattan and had a chance to rest. We finished at about seven. To the point: supper was the only meal at which we ate meat.

Do the arithmetic: Six hours after 7 P.M. is 1 A.M. But I usually went to bed by 10 P.M. (at the latest). Hence, an hour-glass quandary.

Various solutions were bandied about: First, it was suggested that I, alone, would eat a *milchig* supper—either fish, pasta, or cereal. But among the thousands of rules governing *kashrut*, there was one that stated unequivocally that a *milchig* meal and a *fleishig* meal could not be eaten at the same time at the same table--even if no individual ate a taste of both. Furthermore, Mom noted that keeping the dishes and silverware separate would be a organizational nightmare. So that idea was voted down swiftly and unanimously.

The next proposal was to ask our rabbi for a health waiver. But that was quickly resisted for a flurry of reasons: Mom objected to any suggestion that I wasn't healthy; there would be no easy way, were the rabbi to reject our petition, for us to be able follow our best instincts anyway; and the real concern—despite the promise of privacy, was that soon the entire nosey *shul* would know of our dilemma which, Mom insisted, was none of their business.

But, as always, Mom found the solution: At the 10 P.M. quaffing, I would be given only one-half a glass, four ounces carefully measured. The half-glass that I did *not* drink would be in deference to the sacred, historic six-hour rule. Thereby our family complied with all the *kashrut* regulations, and no one would ever be the wiser.

A few years later, in the 7th or 8th grade, when I began Introductory Algebra, I suggested a modification: I would be given only a half-portion of meat at dinner: then the portion of meat that I did *not* eat could be matched with the half-glass of milk that I actually drank (hence no violation); and the half-portion that I did eat could be matched with the half-glass of milk that I did not drink (again, no violation).

Mom said that our original way to doing things was just fine, and that my suggested modification was too cute and too tricky and might tend to make a joke out of what had been a very workable compromise--with no one ever the wiser.

As I think about it now, some seventy years later, I consider Mom's feat all the more amazing, because it is surely easier, astrophysically speaking, to alter the course of the sun than, theologically speaking, to alter the rules of *kashrut*.

WALDBAUM'S ON CONEY ISLAND AVENUE

Some have protested that the president's proposal to raise the federal minimum wage to nine dollars an hour is too modest. But compared to the first hourly minimum wage established by the Fair Labor Standards Act in 1938—25 cents—Mr. Obama's beneficiaries will feel like hedge-fund tycoons, even adjusting for inflation.

Back in the '30s every penny counted, and every penny *was* counted. Mom surveyed the neighborhood's supermarkets far and wide and concluded that Waldbaum's offered the best prices and values. So even though that market was located on distant Coney Island Avenue, equivalent to East 11th Street, and we lived on Ocean Avenue, equivalent to East 20th Street, that extra carrying distance was considered to be well worth it. I don't remember if shopping carts had yet been invented or whether housewives had to carry and not roll their overflowing bundles.

To demonstrate how carefully calibrated Mom's decision was, a rival store on East 15th Street—much closer to home—was popularly referred to as the *gonif* because its prices on many items were higher than Waldbaum's by one penny or sometimes, on a very expensive product, by two. Moral judgments, although finely tuned, were unforgiving.

One would expect a person so designated to be some kind of outlaw, wearing a mask and being quick on the draw. But Mr. Silver was so gentle and accommodating that he almost made the label *gonif* into an honorable one, at least in the Midwood section of Brooklyn. And sometimes, to frustrate the local lexicographer even more, he would announce a sale that *under-priced* Waldbaum's by a penny— and that was a temptation that no shopper could resist. Even so, in the stubborn way of language (does anyone know where Avenue of the Americas is located?), the *gonif* he remained until he retired in the early '50s.

The woman of the house had to shop about three times a week because refrigeration was so limited. In the early '30s, we had a small ice-box that fit neatly into a small alcove; the ice-man, tongs in hand, made regular visits to replace our frozen water supply. I can't imagine what happened in the summer.

When, in later years, an electric refrigerator was installed—a Frigidaire—it had to snuggle into that same tight space. And it came attached with a particular worry for me: Did the light that was on when the door was opened stay on when the door was closed? I was concerned because whenever a bulb had been left on inadvertently anywhere in the apartment, Mom would rebuke the offender by noting that "Edison is rich enough". I was, therefore, relieved when it was demonstrated that the fridge light turned off automatically whenever the fridge door was closed although I assumed that the electric company was disappointed.

A family concern was whether meat products and milk products could share the same refrigerator shelf. We had been advised that some of our more Orthodox neighbors avoided that quandary by having two refrigerators, but that solution exceeded both our space and our wealth. There was even some idle speculation about how the very Orthodox treated Passover, and whether they really had four refrigerators. But idle speculation aside, we squeezed refrigerator items in wherever they would, almost, fit and observed the rules of being kosher only in the eating.

In a neighborhood that was as homogenous as a vat of mashed potatoes, shopping at Waldbaum's provided an unexpected lesson in diversity. There were three or four check-out counters, each manned by a young African-American, then Negro, in his late teenage or early twenties. Each wore a white Waldbaum's apron and each sported a large yellow pencil behind his ear. After the customer placed all of her purchases on the counter, the clerk plucked an appropriate-sized brown bag from a shelf below and wrote the price of each item on that bag in a large, round hand. When the last item had been recorded, he drew a line with a flourish and then, instantaneously, in a fraction of a nano-second, he entered the total—even if there were thirty items. He did not add the columns as I had been taught at P.S. 152; he just wrote down the amount owed. And then he put each item into the bag or bags, and waved on the next customer. Mom, a trained bookkeeper, said that those men were mathematical wizards who should be in college.

Nonetheless, as soon as she unpacked, Mom would check and recheck the arithmetic; no error was ever detected. Sometimes I would be given that task; if my calculation showed a difference, I did it again until I got it right. My worry was that I might find that we had been undercharged. What would we do then? That, I thought, would put our religion to the test. Fortunately, it never happened.

The country may be lurching toward a minimum wage of $9.00 an hour, but growing up in the '30s has left its mark. I'm still tempted to buy two boxes of cereal for the special sale price of $7.00 when the regular price for one box is $3.75. And I don't even like Grape Nuts.

DASHING THROUGH THE SNOW

I am tone-deaf, and once upon a time, back in the 1930s and 1940s, that led to a conundrum of epic, even Talmudic, proportions.

Every year, immediately after Thanksgiving, P.S. 152, in step with the rest of the country, shifted into a Christmas mode. And every year, just after Thanksgiving, my father would write a letter to my teacher, asking that I be excused from singing Christmas carols. And every year, just a few moments after that, I would explain to my father why such a letter was unnecessary.

Such a letter was unnecessary because I had been classified as a "listener", which meant that I had been asked not to join in any class sing-alongs because my voice was *so* off-key that it disoriented everybody else. But being so designated was not punitive or negative at all; in fact, I rather enjoyed the status because I considered singing to be a girl's activity, and that particular disability made me feel more macho, enhancing my secret dream of becoming a famous athlete, probably a record-setting miler.

My point to Dad was that my teacher *already* knew that I would not be singing Christmas carols; therefore, any such correspondence was pointless. It was, I noted, a matter of basic physics: It is not possible *not* to sing twice at the same time—once for reasons that were musical and once for reasons that were theological.

Ignoring Einstein, or whoever it was who proved that two things cannot occupy the exact same space at the exact same time, that annual missive was always dispatched to school, and I was always its reluctant bearer.

Not one to give up, I pursued the subject by asking my father if, as a hypothetical matter, he would object to my singing a holiday song that had absolutely no religious reference, citing, for example, *Jingle Bells*.

His response was that since he could not possibly know every word of every paragraph of every song, the only safe practice would be for me not to sing any carol.

Still not one to give up, I replied by singing—reciting, really—all the *Jingle Bells* lyrics:

> Dashing through the snow
> In a one-horse open sleigh
> O'er the hills we go
> Laughing all the way
> (Through to the end)
> A sleighing song tonight.

There was, I suggested, nothing about Christmas or the New Testament; in fact, I argued, there was nothing that could not be sung with gusto in Hebrew School.

That prompted a hypothetical counter-proposal: If children in Hebrew School would sing *Jingle Bells*, would my class at P.S. 152 sing the non-religious Chanukah song, *I Have A Little Dradel*?

I have a little dradel
I made it out of clay
And when we all are ready
A dradel we will play.

I knew that such ecumenical bliss did not exist, and surely not in my neighborhood. But I wondered why even music, an art form without words, had to be part of sectarian divisions.

The Christmas carol dilemma ended when I graduated from elementary school because there were no class sing-alongs in Midwood High School.

Many years later, I heard discussions of whether the Israeli Philharmonic Orchestra should play compositions by Wagner; some questioned whether any Jewish musicians should participate in performances of Beethoven's *Missa Solemnis* or Bach's *Mass in B Minor*; and I remember one elderly man expressing disappointment that Leonard Bernstein would be conducting *The Messiah*.

Whenever I heard such talk I would think back to my days at P.S. 152 and wish that I had been brave enough to have participated in *Jingle Bells*, but in *sotto voce* of course, so as not to have disoriented my classmates.

BEFORE AND AFTER

The first serious issue I had to resolve about Jesus was not concerned with theology or genealogy, but, rather, with something even more timeless—chronology.

The problem began at the beginning of the 8th Grade, when we were introduced to our first Shakespeare play, *Julius Caesar*. The historical background notes that preceded the text explained that the real Julius Caesar—general, statesman, dictator, writer, and the man who defiantly crossed the Rubicon--was assassinated in the Roman Senate on March 15, 44 B.C.

In my home and in Hebrew School, dates in the ancient world were always B.C.E.

My father was a vigilante when it came to guarding against any perceived Christian infiltration into our public school curriculum, and I wondered what his reaction would be to that otherwise bland introduction. Should I point it out or let it just slip by? It was, after all, a rather insignificant date in a schoolboy's backpack of momentous events—1066, 1492, 1620, 1776, 1789, 1812, 1860. (Note: We were just reaching the Civil War.)

Either course was risky: If I brought it to his attention, might he cause an embarrassing fuss by writing one of his pointed letters to the school authorities; or worse still, might he involve our rabbi and local politicians, always eager for an issue? But if I ignored it, would I be guilty of failing to protect the Jewish people in their hour of need right in my own neighborhood? As I had learned from my recent reading, Spinoza had been excommunicated for a lot less.

What really confused me was when I asked Dad the first time what "B.C.E." meant, and he replied, "Before the Common Era". I pressed on, and asked what the Common Era was, and he answered that it was the time as measured from the birth of Christ.

That surprised me, because it meant that "B. C." and "B.C.E." were identical—both acknowledged Jesus as the beginning—so why the alphabetical gyration?

It occurred to me that if Jews wanted to escape the calendar's acknowledgement of Jesus, they should measure everything, instead, from the birth of Moses. According to Biblical scholars, who calculated the time of the Exodus, Moses was born about 3,500 years ago (or, as the text I read put it, about 1556 B.C.E.) And if Moses's birthday were used, there would be no need to divide world events between "before" and "after" since almost everything would be after.

I then realized that it would be easier still if the world just adopted the Hebrew calendar, which in my 8th Grade stood at a neat 5700. By definition, since that was when the world began (see

Genesis), nothing *could* have preceded it, eliminating for all time the need to use a before designation.

If a religiously neutral calendar was the goal, perhaps the world should adopt the Chinese lunar version, which was accepted by Buddhists, Taoists and Confucians alike, giving it wide support throughout Asia. But I worried that their use of symbolic animals—Dragon, Horse, Snake, Goat—to designate the years might be off-putting for all Westerners, whether religious or not. Demarking any holiday, religious or national, as, for instance, the Year of the Snake would not be acceptable to anyone I knew.

My various plans to eliminate the use of both B.C. and B.C.E. in order to protect Jewish integrity ended when, shortly later, I was given a Jewish history textbook which recorded that the destruction of the Second Temple occurred on the 9th day of Av (Tishah b'Av) in the year 70 A.D.

ABRAHAM'S SECRET

My parents directed their most withering scorn at families who ended their sons' Hebrew School education immediately after their Bar Mitzvahs: "Just when they're *finally* beginning to learn something."

That sharp criticism embarrassed me after February 6, 1943, the date of my own coming-of-age ceremony, for how I longed to be free of those three dreary weekly sessions—Monday and Wednesday afternoons, rushing there pell-mell after classes ended at P.S. 152 and every Sunday morning. But it took me a few years of quiet, sullen anguish before I was able to gather the courage to complain. And when I was finally liberated, it was the fortuitous result of my own overwhelming incompetence.

It all began when I was sent to Hebrew School at age seven. That curriculum had two subjects, language and Bible; I understood neither equally. They could as well have sent me to Hebrew University to audit lectures on Spinoza. By contrast, most of my classmates were in the nine-to-ten age bracket, and that spread made all the difference.

The Hebrew language course introduced something new, an alphabet with strange squiggles; and stranger still, it went from right to left, and why, I wondered, but not out loud, did the Jews always have to be so contrary. After a while, with studious drilling, I was able to sound the words, even when I had no idea what they meant, and that made me wonder, but not out loud, if I was really reading. It is now some seventy years later, and I'm still troubled by that dilemma.

The study of the Bible was mystifying. We began with The Book of Genesis (*Berashis*) to learn how the world *(olum)* began: It all began, it seems, with God creating the Earth in six days and resting on the seventh. It was one of the few parts of the Bible that I under-stood because if God didn't rest on the Sabbath, who would? But the teacher's explanation that those numbers were meta-fours was beyond my reach; even though I was good in arithmetic, I could not figure out how that particular four fit into either six or seven. But I knew enough not to ask.

Next on our biblical agenda came a cast of characters—A begot B who begot C who begot D who begot E, down through a lot of generations, all compressed into a few paragraphs filled with names I had never heard of. Was I supposed to know who they were or memorize them in their correct ancestral order? Those people came and went so fast—it was like flipping the pages of a telephone book— that I decided to ignore them and hope or pray, pray really, that they'd not be on a test. Then I had this thought: if we had used the modern edition of the Bible, would the list possibly include some of my own relatives from several generations back, especially someone from Vilna where my Mom's family had been prominent?

While writing this essay, I thought I'd check to see if my fading memory was accurate, and right there in Genesis (5:6-28) Seth begot Enos who begot Kenan who begot Mahalalel who begot Jared who begot Enoch who begot Methuselah who begot Lameck who begot Noah. That's why I gave up trying to memorize them.

Our study continued with the story of Abraham being 100 years old and his wife Sarah 90 when their son Isaac was born. Genesis then recorded that Abraham, after having waited a century for a child was, nonetheless, ready to sacrifice the lad just to please God. That made me nervous—if that is what made God happy, I surely didn't want to make Him sad.

My Bar Mitzvah came and went, and I struggled with my conscience about how best to present a case for my liberation. I had been reading that some degree of teenage rebellion was normal, even expected, but I understood, too, that those Fourth of July sentiments did not extend to religion, certainly not in Brooklyn, and particularly not in my family.

When I entered high school the world became more exciting; and those dreary sessions were an ever greater drag. I realized just how little Hebrew I actually knew after seven years, and I was embarrassed.

One evening, after supper, I blurted out what had been stirring for many months.

"Mom, I'm quitting Hebrew School. I've learned practically nothing."

"Mordecai, whose fault is that?"

All my intricate plans seemed crushed at that moment since I knew exactly whose fault it was.

Then there was a sudden bit of old-fashioned Divine Intervention: my parents were so upset by my proposed disengagement that they scheduled an appointment for me to meet with the rabbi and the Hebrew School principal. I had never looked neater, with a shirt and a tie and a black skullcap in my pocket in case it was required since we were to meet in the rabbi's austere study. I was petrified. What could I say? That I would do better in the future? That I'd try harder? That I'd do extra reading to perfect my Hebrew? I could say anything, but they knew and I knew that nothing would change, and that my parents would just have to resign themselves to the general opinion that I was no Maimonides.

That led to the rabbi's unexpected suggestion that I drop out of the Hebrew curriculum and register in the Sunday School program instead, to study Jewish history and traditions, all in English, and just once a week.

It was a stunning and unanticipated result, the very best example in all history of the phrase "ignorance is bliss".

But now that I'm an octogenarian, I have one regret about having left that Bible class so early—I never learned Abraham's secret for eternal youth.

BLINKERED

The Kwakiutl Indians of centuries ago are considered to have been the exemplars of ethnocentrism because they believed that the sun's only mission was to rise and set over *their* sacred ancestral lands; other tribes would have to fend for themselves.

But compared to the range of vision in my home in Brooklyn in the 1930s and 1940s, those Kwakiutl Indians were world federalists. My parents' narrowness was not based on any heavenly orbit, but on a more earthly focus: They related everything, or almost everything, to being Jewish.

Mom had no interest in sports and did not know first base from a first down, but she was a loyal fan of baseball great Hank Greenberg, football great Sid Luckman, who lived in the neighborhood, and cheered for Goody Rosen, the Dodgers' mediocre center-fielder:

Mom, he's just ordinary—at best.

Mordecai, if they'd give him a chance he'd be a star because he's probably very smart.

Although they rarely went to the movies, they idolized Edward G. Robinson because his real name was Emanuel Goldenberg, John Garfield because his real name was Julius Garfinkl and Paul Muni because his real name was Meshilam Meier Weisenfreund. I asked why some had changed their names, and the response was that Hollywood studios liked names that were short and could fit onto movie marquees. I decided not to mention Olivia de Havilland.

Of course they loved to mention Albert Einstein and the fact that he had once been refused a Nobel Prize because he was Jewish. When I countered that Isaac Newton was not, Mom said that you couldn't be sure because so many people back then hid their true identities. Anyway, she noted, Jonas Salk was.

There was a continuing controversy over Christopher Columbus. Some suggested that he must have been Jewish because August 2, 1492, the very day that he set sail for what would be his discovery of America, was also the very day that the Jews were required by the Inquisition to leave Spain: "Such a coincidence would be too remarkable if Columbus himself wasn't Jewish." Years later, when I read *The Great Explorers* by Samuel Eliot Morrison, I learned that Columbus was probably an anti-Semite, but there was no point in raising that point so belatedly.

A sketch of Louis D. Brandeis hung on our living room wall, and there were two biographies of him in our modest library—two books I still own. Dad noted that although he was "as brilliant as

Aristotle and as wise as Solomon," the President of Harvard opposed his nomination to the Supreme Court anyway.

And on and on and on. In music it was George Gershwin, Irving Berlin, Richard Rodgers, Jerome Kern, Benny Goodman and even Artie Shaw, and on and on; Aaron Copland of *Rodeo* fame was some- times lassoed into the discussion.

Finally, one day I asked Mom about Louis Lepke and Benjamin Bugsy Siegel, the founders of Murder, Inc, the most reprehensible gangsters in the world, and about Meyer Lansky, co-chairman with Lucky Luciano of the National Crime Syndicate. All, I noted, were synagogue regulars.

She wasn't nonplussed at all, not for an instant. Rather, she reiterated that they were all very smart people—very smart—who, unfortunately, had been led astray. The real problem, she explained, was Prohibition:

Prohibition bred crime and criminals. If it hadn't been for
Prohibition they'd all probably have been doctors or lawyers
or famous composers because they were all very talented people.

I noted, cautiously, that even after Prohibition ended, those lads continued on their rampant murderous ways. But Mom ignored that

that response, and continued to focus, as always, on their keen intelligence:

> They must have been very smart people to have outwitted
> the police for all those years.

Mom, they didn't outwit anybody. They bribed people and murdered people.

Mordecai, if colleges hadn't discriminated against Jews they'd all have gone to Oxford or Harvard.

Where they might have majored in anthropology, proving Mom correct that the Kwakiutl Indians were probably Jewish—their name does have an undeniable Eastern European ring, perhaps from a shtetl just south of Vilna. And then, as landsmen, we'd all be happy to share their—our—bespoke solar rays.

THE DAILY SWITCH

The world was a mixed-up, confusing place in the winter of 1942-1943, especially to someone 13 years old. I wasn't sure if Russia was friend or foe, if Stalin was a monster or a hero, if President Roosevelt's unprecedented third term was wise or dangerous, or if the American and Allied armies could, somehow, reverse the frightening course of the war.

In the context of those mighty events, my Dad's switch from the *New York Times* to the *Herald-Tribune* was not historic. But it made a huge impression on me, one which I still remember more than seventy years later.

My father was a man of habit, and he was no more likely to abandon his daily reading of the *Times* than he would abandon his pipe or chained gold pocket-watch.

But he explained that the *Times* had to be abandoned because it deliberately and scandalously refused to acknowledge the desperate plight of European Jewry. The *Trib*, by contrast, reported that grim news honestly, completely and, most importantly, with passion.

I was amazed, because until then the only things I knew about the *Trib* was that its owner, Ogden Reid, was a member of high WASP society, that its readers lived on the Upper East Side of

Manhattan or in Connecticut or both, and that most had direct links to the *Mayflower*. And now, in our home, Mr. Reid was suddenly considered to be a hero, almost up there with Hank Greenberg, Benny Goodman and Henry Morgenthau. It was particularly memorable because it was the first time that I had ever heard my father praise a Gentile. Until then he had agreed with the neighborhood's unanimous opinion that scratch a Gentile, any Gentile, even the most virtuous, and just beneath his skin you would find a sword-wielding Cossack in pogrom mode.

I was more confused. Wasn't the *Times* owned by Jews?

Dad's response was complicated: The *Times* was owned by German Jews who had come to the United States a tad earlier than the rest of us, in the 1850s and 1860s, and by now, the 1940s, considered themselves to be pure-bred American with nary a Semitic trace. But lest someone question their loyalty, they did contortions "like Houdini" so that nobody could ever accuse the *Times* of being a Jewish newspaper with a Jewish slant. And so they simply ignored all Jewish news, no matter how newsworthy.

But, his monologue continued, the courageous Mr. Reid and the *Trib* had no such complex.

I was more confused, a lot more confused: Weren't the German Jews the very focal point of our concern? Weren't they the very victims of Nazi brutality? How could *we* be piling on *them*?

The explanation became digressive, but it seemed to boil down to this: The German Jews in the United States were different than the German Jews in Germany because those who had come here had assimilated, but those who had stayed in Germany had remained more steadfast in their Judaism.

I reacted with surprise: If those who assimilated had done so well and those who remained loyal had all been destroyed, assimilating did seem to be the wiser choice, surely the safer one.

My father replied that I had missed the point, which was that the Nazis murdered all the Jews, whether religious or atheistic or somewhere in between, and that it was the journalistic responsibility of the *Times* to report that fairly and completely. But they failed in that duty because the German Jews who owned it had censored it. And they censored it because they were so uncomfortable in their Jewishness.

Since I was already considered by my family to be a likely renegade on religious matters even though I conformed to all the rules and performed all my required sacred duties, I thought it wise to desist. But it did seem to me that those German Jews in America had done remarkably well. And, of course, everyone in our neighborhood voted for Herbert Lehman every time he ran for Governor of New York or the United States Senate. He was then considered to be Jewish, without any geographical designation or limitation.

Our family, including me, stayed loyal to the *Herald-Tribune* until its sad demise in 1966. And a wonderful newspaper it was. It brought into our home such distinguished writers as Red Smith (the best sportswriter ever, and one of the country's finest essayists, ever), Walter Kerr (a theater critic with remarkable insight who wrote brilliantly) and Walter Lippmann (considered the wisest political commentator and theorist of his time although his style was opaque and his subjects boring).

After the War the Jewish community did deep soul-searching about who could have done more to have prevented the Holocaust. Among those blamed whether deservedly or not was Walter Lippmann. It was said that he ignored all entreaties that he use his vast influence with President Roosevelt and the State Department to intercede on behalf of his fellow Jews trapped in Europe.

My father had no information one way or another, but he did

note that the rumors were probably "almost surely" true since Walter Lippmann, who graduated from Harvard in 1909, was from that same German-Jewish upper class that owned the *Times*.

For a balanced presentation, there is also an exculpatory theory—that although Lippmann *wrote* for the *Trib*, he might well have been a *reader* of the *Times*--and in that case he can't possibly be blamed, for he would have had no way of knowing.

THE ELUSIVE POWER OF PRAYER

Growing up in a moderately religiously observant home, nothing was more mysterious to me than God and how to worship Him. What, I wondered, did prayers achieve, particularly the ones that I recited in Hebrew by rote without knowing exactly what they meant? Of course, since God understood Hebrew, it really didn't matter if *I* understood it or not. But it did concern me that since I did not know exactly what I was asking for, I would never know if my prayers had been answered.

It was a given, of course, that the Jewish People had some sort of special link to the Almighty, which meant that if I could only get it right I would be among the favored. The complication was that there were at least five separate branches of Judaism in our own tight Brooklyn neighborhood, and each had not only its own particular ways, but each seemed to be so hostile to all the others. Which led to another nervous doubt: What if our family's branch, the Conservative, was not the true one? Would all of my prayers, including the rote ones, have been in vain?

What were those internecine differences that divided Jewish worship into warring camps? While we, as expressed by my father, considered our Conservative practice to be a perfect blend of tradition and modernity, we were less generous to the others:

The Orthodox were considered to be too rigid, "too fixed in the 18th Century." Sometimes, when being particularly dismissive, my father would chase them back to the 17th. Despite that negative characterization, I learned that we, the Conservatives, and they, the Orthodox, used the identical prayer books on both the Sabbath and on the holidays. So how different, spiritually, could those two branches really be? When I timidly inquired, the main point in response was that in our services men and women sat together, whereas in the Orthodox they were separated. That did not seem to me to be a difference that God would care about, but I also knew that I was too young to understand the full nature of the male-female relationship.

The Reform were described as too lax, too indifferent to the power of fervent prayer, "too much like Unitarians." Since I confused *Unitarian* with *utilitarian,* I assumed that the Reform were out of religious step because they were too practical. And since worship and daily chores were, by definition, inconsistent, I thought that opposition to the Reform made perfect doctrinal sense.

There was sharp criticism of the Reconstructionists for being too haughty. It was said that you could not hear a Reconstructionist sermon without having to look up at least five words in an unabridged dictionary; and that each rabbi considered himself to be a professor of philosophy at Oxford. When I learned later that the founder of

Reconstructionism was Mordecai Kaplan I had a softer opinion since I was always partial to someone named "Mordecai". Not a very philosophical point, but it was my firm position anyway.

The largest denomination in Judaism, by far, were the Irreligious. We, as expressed by my father, had contempt for them as people who were ashamed of being Jewish or who were just plain ignorant of their own history. Most of our neighbors happened to fit neatly into that category—and they were, for the most part, very nice individuals; that made me wonder if being religious made a person better or more moral. When I posed that question to my father he surprised me by his candid response:

No, religious people aren't better or more moral than irreligious people.

Why then be religious?

It's a bond that links the generations, a bond that goes back thousands of years.

Do you have to believe in God to be part of that chain?

The Orthodox would say "Yes", but I'm not sure.

Since being a Believer did not make one a better person, I suggested that perhaps there was no reason for me to continue to go to services every Friday night and every Saturday morning.

But my father saw it differently, like one of those rabbis from the 18th Century. Make it the 17th.

A TWIST OF FAITH

There were four bakeries on Avenue J in the Midwood Section of Brooklyn when I was growing up in the 1930s and 1940s: Elfenbein's, where we shopped, Stern's, Steinberg's (I'm not sure of that name, but it was something like that) and Ebinger's.

On many Thursday evenings, at supper, the same question was discussed: Where to buy our *Shabbos* challah? In 1946, when I was a high school junior, that question suddenly took on a new dimension: Should they—my Mom and Dad—ruin my chances of going to Harvard?

Mom suggested that the point was ridiculous since my chance of being admitted to Harvard was about a million to one. To which Dad, always precise—he had been a business major in college-- added that it was a more like 100 million to one. To which I added that as bad as those odds seemed, they—my own Mom and Dad-- were, unnecessarily and arbitrarily, making them a whole lot worse.

The choice of where to buy the challah was always between Elfenbein's, our regular baker, and Ebinger's, a bakery famous, at least on Avenue J, for its unrivaled excellence. An Ebinger chocolate cup-cake was the reward for a good report card.

Since it was agreed that Ebinger's was the best—"by far," interjected Dad—the issue boiled down to whether I should be sent to

Elfenbein's nevertheless, because a challah was not just a loaf of bread. Rather, reflected Dad, it had a spiritual significance that had linked the Jewish people over the centuries; in every time and place, Jews, whether rich or poor, whether observant or indifferent, sanctified the *Shabbos* by eating challah. Therefore, he concluded, buying a challah from a *goyisher* bakery when a Jewish bakery was available was spiritually wrong.

I then raised the college issue. If Jews argued that colleges should admit students strictly on merit, and that one's religion should not be a factor, weren't we being hypocritical by buying our challah at Elfenbein's when Ebinger's product was acknowledged to be superior?

Mom suggested that I was wasting time with such a discussion because the Harvard Admissions Office would never know that I went to Elfenbein's to buy our challah, and even if somehow they did find out, they'd never know the reason.

I persisted—but *we'd* know.

Mom then put a new and more literal twist on the discussion—if being admitted to Harvard depended on where we bought our challah, did that admissions office also take into account where we bought our seeded rye, pumpernickel, whole wheat or sourdough?

And if so, then Harvard wasn't worth applying to in the first place. She wondered out loud: Didn't that college have requirements that were more academically relevant and less yeast-related?

I tried to explain that I was using our challah purchase only as an example, a metaphor, to demonstrate our double-standard. But I realized that she understood that very well, but was just pushing on to be crusty.

Dad sometimes proposed a compromise—we'd buy the challah at Stern's, which was almost as good as Ebinger's, if not quite. But Mom objected, noting that she never liked Stern's because their cakes were too rich, especially their whipped-cream toppings. I argued that since we weren't buying Stern's cakes, it didn't matter how rich they were, but that logic, which seemed to me to be conclusive, was ignored, and Mom ruled out Stern's peremptorily. And anyway, she said, Stern's was too expensive, which, I suspected, was probably the real reason we never shopped there in the first place.

There was also the side issue of whether the challah should be round or elliptical with braids. Dad favored the round shape because it represented the Earth and the Heavens, and what was *Shabbos* but an appreciation of the wonders of God's universe. Mom preferred the twist because slices were smaller, and there was less waste, so the twist was what I was usually instructed to buy. But either shape, round or elliptical, I never had that bread sliced at the bakery, even though its new electric slicing machine was a wondrous sign of modernity. Dad said that slicing the challah was part of the *kiddush* ceremony, and I had to agree with him. Indeed, he used a special knife that was sheathed in velvet and had a decorated blade and a decorated porcelain handle that included a Hebrew inscription. Except for the writing the design could have been Persian.

No, I didn't get into Harvard. I didn't even apply. When my own parents put the spirituality of a loaf of bread ahead of my education I knew that it was time to switch to atheism, but secretly of course, a Marrano in reverse.

A STOCKBOY'S DILEMMA

In my last two years of high school, 1946 and 1947, I had a priceless possession—-a summer job. I was a stockboy at the Hebrew Publishing Company, 77-79 Delancey Street, New York.

It was a company that my scholarly and distinguished maternal grandfather (born in Vilna in 1865; died in New York in 1920) had helped to organize in 1901. His picture, one of several on the far wall, still overlooked the company's office, and his presence, or so it seemed to me, continued to be felt.

In the 1940s the company was a leading manufacturer of Hebrew New Year cards, and since the occasion to be celebrated fell in September or October, summer was the busy season for manufacture and distribution.

The company's catalogue listed about thirty-five card designs; each was separately packaged in boxes of twenty. The boxes of each design had their own separate spaces on the back shelves, and it was the stockboy's task to pluck the right boxes to match the order sheet.

Then others, more highly skilled still, were responsible for wrapping, addressing and shipping.

There were five or six stockboys, and all of them wore a yarmulke—except me. In fact, every other male employee of the company—salesmen and executives of all ranks—also wore a yarmulke.

On the second or third day on the job, one of those elders took me aside and inquired, discreetly, how it was that I was bare-headed. I replied that I was not orthodox. Whereupon he asked me if I thought that I was smarter than my grandfather.

That was a hard question for a 16 ½ year-old because I was determined not to be trapped into wearing a skullcap. I was slow to respond because I tried to calculate where a *Yes* answer and a *No* answer would lead, a few exchanges later; but I was as lost as a novice chess player.

When I felt that the time had run out, and that I would have to say something, I said that no, I was not smarter than my grandfather. And than I added, in almost a whisper, because I had to have the last word, that Einstein was smarter still and he didn't wear a yarmulke either.

The instant that I uttered that addition I knew I had made a mistake, setting up, I was sure, his derisive rejoinder: "Mordecai, are you comparing yourself to Albert Einstein already?"

But instead my interrogator spoke philosophically and softly:

> Einstein may know more about the planets and the
> stars and other material things that are millions—
> some say billions—-of miles away, but your grandfather
> knew more about the heavens and things that are
> holy and spiritual, things that are inside of us, our
> very souls. Einstein may have been, as you say, smarter
> than your grandfather, but I think that your grandfather was
> much the wiser.

That quiet, lyrical response overwhelmed me; I had expected something more contentious, more stridently religious. He said that I should think about it, that we'd continue our discussion in a few days.

And there was a lot to think about. I was an innocent high school junior, and now I was suddenly enmeshed in an endless controversy, centuries old, between science and religion—two subjects that I knew very little about, except for the very basics: that Galileo had been right and Ptolemy wrong because the Earth circled the sun (General Science I); and that the Red Sea had parted, or how else would the Hebrews have escaped from Egypt--although that may have been metaphorical. (Exodus 14:16-22).

Although brilliant and articulate advocates have participated in the debate over the years--on the science side there have been doubters like Richard Dawkins and Richard Feynman, and on the spiritual side believers like Rabbi Lord Jonathan Sachs and Rowan Williams, the Archbishop of Canterbury--but to my mind, nobody has posed the issue more neatly or more poetically than did that mid-level employee in the summer of 1946.

When we resumed a few afternoons later he was disappointed that I was still uncovered. I replied that I had been thinking a lot about what he had said, and had a lot more thinking to do. He answered that I was doing the right thing, that thinking such things through carefully was the only way to come to a meaningful conclusion about something so profound, and that my grandfather would be proud of me whatever I decided.

That disarmed me totally because I expected a lecture noting how strange it was, how ironic, that I, a founder's grandson, was the only one not properly dressed.

As I brooded about that I suddenly became wary that I was being shrewdly out-maneuvered by someone much more experienced than I in discussing the place of religion in one's private life. I had been challenged before for my disinterest in things sacred, but never so sweetly.

It was a dilemma—should I wear a yarmulke, if only while working at the company, under my grandfather's very gaze (the compromise he suggested), or should I continue my impious way?

I chose to be impious, and so remain. Whether that was the right call or not I won't know until it is too late to change.

THE TALMUD AND EBBETS FIELD

When the Dodger right-hander, Ed Head, went to the mound on Monday afternoon, April 23, 1946, to pitch against the Boston Braves, he had no reason to suspect that the game would be enmeshed in several thought-stirring Talmudic conundrums.

The first involved my very right to go to Ebbets Field that particular day. I was then a junior at Midwood High but was home from school in deference to the last day of Passover. A few of my friends, who had also stayed home, decided to see the game, which in those days began at 3 P.M. My parents suggested that it was improper and unethical for me to stay home from classes in order to observe a Jewish holiday and then go to the ballpark. I replied that I had dutifully attended services that morning, even staying to the end, enduring not only the rabbi's predictable sermon, but all the repetitious prayers that had followed. Therefore, I argued, I had fully discharged all my religious obligations and was free to enjoy the rest of the day.

When my parents disagreed, of course, I offered a compromise: I would walk to Ebbets Field, an exercise that would take about fifty minutes, rather than take the Ocean Avenue trolley. It was a foolish gesture since in our observant but not Orthodox home, riding on Passover was allowed.

Nonetheless, in the mysterious way of theological discourse, my offer was accepted—but with a proviso: I was *not* to visit my paternal grandma, who lived on Eastern Parkway, just a few steps from the ballpark:

> There is no reason for grandma to know that
> you went to the ballgame on Pesach. The fewer
> people who know the better. And we certainly
> don't want Aunt Essie or Aunt Florence [my father's
> two irreligious sisters] to know because then we'd
> never hear the end of it.

Since visiting grandma was more duty than pleasure, that edict was readily agreed to. But it did raise another moral issue: If I was permitted to go to the game, why couldn't I tell people, especially since I was going with several talkative friends so that the secret would soon be known far and wide without my revealing it. But my parents adhered to their rule, especially about grandma--If others found out it could not be helped, but *I* was to tell no one. Their logic made no sense to me, but since I would be going to the game and not visiting grandma there was surely no reason to argue any further.

My friends and I walked to Ebbets Field, paid 55 cents for our bleacher seats, and were rewarded for our impiety by being treated to one of baseball's rarest glories, a no-hitter. Ed Head and the Dodgers won 5-0.

My father had listened to the game on the radio; the moment I returned home, my parents greeted me with a stern reminder that I was not allowed to tell *anyone* about my extraordinary adventure.

That prompted still another Talmudic puzzle: Why would the Almighty reward such irreverence, particularly since none of my friends had attended the synagogue that morning, by providing us with a pitching feat so grand?

The only explanation my parents could offer was the usual lame one—the Almighty acts in mysterious ways. But I absorbed His stern lesson at once: witnessing a no-hitter but not being allowed to tell was a punishment that was profound.

And Ed Head probably thought that his no-hitter was due to his pitching skill.

THE DIPLOMA

In the early spring of 1951, my senior year at college, the dean sent a letter to all members of the graduating class advising how our names would appear on our diplomas. If anyone had a problem, his office had to be contacted at once because our names were to be hand-printed by a calligrapher, which meant that no corrections could be made once that elegant, artistic inscription had begun.

My first name was listed as *Mordicai*, an obvious error. Following the instructions, I immediately advised the dean's office, in a hand-delivered note, that the correct spelling of my first name was *Mordecai*.

A few moments later I was summoned by the dean himself, who explained that the college's spelling was correct because *Mordicai* was how my name appeared on the birth certificate that I had provided when I had matriculated back in 1947; and he pulled it out of a folder to prove his point. I was embarrassed that I had lived with that error, unknowingly, for twenty-one years.

But it was really no problem, he assured me; the college would accept a statement from the registrar at the elementary school where I was first enrolled, certifying how my name was then given. I called Mom, and she immediately marched over to P.S. 152 on Glenwood Road and East 23rd Street, Brooklyn to obtain the corrective. But alas, school was closed for spring vacation.

I reported that delay to the dean, who was surprisingly unsympathetic. When I meekly suggested that my diploma should be put aside temporarily, awaiting the end of the week-long vacation in Brooklyn, he took bureaucracy to a new level, asserting that my diploma, like every other one, had to be done in its proper alphabetic order. There were, he noted, about one thousand diplomas to be prepared, including those for Masters Degree candidates and Ph.Ds. Therefore, he concluded, no variations could be permitted lest the whole process unravel.

His final point was legal: "A diploma, Mordecai, is a legal document and we are unable to change the spelling from your birth certificate even if we wanted to." But he reiterated that an appropriate letter from P.S. 152 would be accepted…if timely.

I protested that after four diligent years I was entitled to a diploma that spelled my name correctly. And where, I asked him, would I display a diploma with such a blatant error?

He would not budge. I asked him to open the Bible—any version of the Bible—to the Book of Esther, and he would understand that there was only one way to spell *Mordecai*. His response was that the Bible was irrelevant, that it could not, unlike the registrar at P.S. 152, overrule my birth certificate.

I next explained that I was an avid *Mordecai* follower, and could recite the names of every famous American who bore that name, and that each one spelled it *Mordecai*. As quick examples I recited Mordecai Lincoln, the President's uncle, and Mordecai Wyatt Johnson, a distinguished theologian and educator--he was president of Howard University--and Three-Fingered Mordecai Brown, the Chicago Cubs' great pitcher. I recounted to him how I told the kids in the schoolyard that I had been named for that baseball Hall of Famer, and how I immediately rose in their esteem, although, of course, I confided, I had been named for a scholarly rabbi from Vilna whose knowledge of balls and strikes was quite limited. And there was Mordecai Kaplan, a famous Jewish scholar and philosopher. Feeling more and more confidant, I noted that the Lincoln Family genealogy was filled with *Mordecais* over many generations.

None of that made any impression because, as he said more than once, he had no doubt how *Mordecai* was spelled.

I thought of going to the college president, or to my congressman or senator, or the press, or to my own family rabbi in Brooklyn, but none of them, in my opinion, would be able to overcome the dean's legal point.

I was about to give up, but was goaded on by his triumphant smirk. And then an idea:

Sir, since a diploma is a legal document, I insist that it bear my entire name.

Of course, Mordecai, that's a proper and fair request. In fact, that is exactly how a diploma must be.

My middle name chances to be my Mother's family name, Katzenellenbogen. You can confirm that in the file.

I did see that that is your Mother's family name, but I didn't know that it was also your middle name.

But it is. Using one's Mother's family name was, for some Jewish families, part of their ancient tradition. And since the diploma is a legal document, I insist that it be accurate.

I'm afraid that your entire name, Mordecai Katzenellenbogen Rosenfeld, will not fit on the diploma, no matter how small the lettering. And since we use only one size diploma, you will have to abandon your middle name.

I can't do that even if I wanted to. A legal document is a legal document.

[A Long Pause]

Mordecai, perhaps we can reach an accommodation. If I agreed to spell *Mordecai* the way it is spelled in the Bible, would you agree to drop your middle name, at least for diploma purposes?

Dean, that seems like a fair and reasonable compromise.

We shook hands, and the graduation exercises went off smoothly.

In retrospect I should have pressed my advantage and insisted on being awarded an honorary degree as well because, more than any of the honorees who had been chosen in1951, I was truly a Man of Letters.

WRESTLING WITH A PRESIDENT

Jacob wrestling with an angel (Genesis 32:23-33) is said to represent each of us grappling with our personal doubts, whatever they are. And if you wrestle with them honestly—and don't deny them—you will prevail.

In that hopeful Biblical spirit, I hereby report that I had been wrestling with President Franklin Delano Roosevelt privately since 1939.

I. 1936

Our relationship began innocently, in 1936, when I was a first-grader at P.S. 152. Our class lined up along Bedford Avenue, one block away, to see and cheer the President, who had come to lay the cornerstone for a new college, Brooklyn College; it was to be built just up the street, on a site sacred to children because it was where the circus had put up its big tent every spring. I can still see him sitting in the back of his open black convertible, wearing his familiar hat and waving. But our class's interest was surely focused more on the accompanying squad of motorcycle police, with their space-man helmets, fierce-looking goggles and polished boots. A president had to be pretty important to merit a dazzling escort like that.

In those years, the mid-1930s, my parents regarded President Roosevelt with reverence, as a man of mythic wonders; that feeling that was reinforced everywhere—in school, at the synagogue, among our neighbors. Being devoted to FDR was part of being a loyal American—a simple formula for a complicated time.

II. May, 1939

In May 1939, the German liner, the *S.S. St. Louis*, carrying 915 Jewish refugees from Europe, reached Florida and safety.

But they were refused entry. And no other country—specifically Cuba and Canada—was persuaded to open any door. They were sent back to Europe and a tragic fate; more than 250 perished in the Holocaust.

The Jewish community was horrified; but it was cautious and hesitant and too nervous and too frightened to criticize the President: "Let's not stir up any more anti-Semitism"; "We're still safe here— thank God"; "Shush, or we'll be accused of dragging America into a war".

Surrounding those Jewish fears, the rest of the neighborhood was ever more loyal to the President. To most people, the *St. Louis* was just another small ship on another routine ocean crossing.

It was a confusing time for a nine-year-old. The atmosphere at P.S. 152 was, of course, of unquestioned devotion to the president who was keeping us out of that never-ending European conflict. But the atmosphere at Hebrew School and the synagogue was sullen with doubts and fears. My parents tried to adhere to both agendas, but it was a closing vise.

III. Passover, 1940

We celebrated the first Seder, every year, with my mother's family, just two blocks away. And every year I had the same two tasks: to carry the *shmura* matzos that my father had bought on the Lower East Side the day before and to recite the Four Questions. But I knew that the Seder that year, 1940, would not be routine.

The discussion of the presidential campaign and an unprecedented third term began a few moments after we arrived; a few seconds later the topic was the *St. Louis*. My Uncle Moe, our host, was our family Republican and was, as far as I knew, perhaps the only Republican in Brooklyn. My father quickly defended the President, arguing that he had surely done everything within his power, albeit quietly behind the scenes, to rescue the Jews, but there were rules and regulations and laws and protocols that had to be respected, that even a president of the United States was limited by the Constitution, which was one of the strengths of our system.

Before I could ask what the word *protocol* meant, my uncle interrupted with a simple response that I have never forgotten: "If there had been 900 cattle aboard every one of them would have been saved."

That verbal punch made President Roosevelt my enemy.

IV 1940-2012

A lot happened in this world between 1940 and 2012. But throughout those years Franklin Delano Roosevelt was always considered to be among our very greatest presidents. I agreed, but with a tiny, faint, mental asterisk. 1939 and the *St. Louis* was long ago; and Jews in America—including myself-- had done remarkably, unbelievably well. It would be petty and captious to complain, and disgracefully ungrateful.

V. The Spring, 2012

Some time during the late spring of 2012, as the presidential election heated up, an old friend insisted that I read *Roosevelt and Hopkins- An Intimate History* by Robert E. Sherwood (Harper Brothers, 1948), and provided me with his tattered copy. Sherwood wrote the book after conducting hundreds of interviews and reviewing many thousands of official and private papers; it is probably the most authoritative book on the intimate inside of the Roosevelt presidency.

My friend's point was to compare the Roosevelt record with Barack Obama's--that FDR had been a magnificent president and President Obama could not compare.

But the book was a rude shock. As I read carefully, I came to the spring of 1939, the time of the voyage of the *St. Louis* (pages 114-117). The events of those days were described in detail—Hopkins had traveled with the President to Warm Springs, Georgia; there was an exchange of messages between the President and Hitler; in June, Washington prepared for a visit from King George VI and Queen Elizabeth, for which Harry Hopkins had to rent a cutaway and striped pants. But the *St. Louis* and the desperate refugees aboard are not even mentioned.

That stirred me to check the index—another shock. The word *Jews* or *Jewish* does not appear; the index goes from *Japan* to *Jewett, Frank B.* to *Johnson, Gerald W.* Nor is the word *Hebrew* included.

As a double-check, I first confirmed that Kristallnacht occurred on November 9-10, 1938. *Roosevelt and Hopkins* discussed many of the events of that very time (pages 98-104)—the congressional elections of 1938, and an attack by the Scripps-Howard newspapers on Senator Alben Barkley (Democrat from Kentucky) and the W.P.A. But Kristallnacht is not even mentioned.

I then parsed the book to see if I could discover *any* reference to the plight of the Jewish People, and I located just two, both distressing: On March 27, 1943, Hopkins convened a small committee to discuss ways to augment the shipment of supplies to Britain and wrote this memo (page 717):

> Hull raised the question of the 60 or 70 thousand Jews that are in Bulgaria and threatened with extermination... Eden replied that the whole problem of the Jews in Europe is very difficult and we should move very cautiously about offering to take all Jews out of a country like Bulgaria. If we do that, then the Jews of the world will be wanting us to make similar offers in Poland and Germany...Furthermore any such mass movement would be very dangerous to security because the Germans would be sure to attempt to put a number of their agents in the group...

The only other reference in the book to the plight of the Jews is concerned with the President's meeting with King Ibn Saud immediately following the Yalta Conference (February 4-11, 1945; pages 871-2). Hopkins wrote:

> And I never could reconcile the President's statement at the press conference later that he had learned more from Ibm Saud about Palestine in five minutes than he had learned in a lifetime— because the only thing he learned which all people concerned with the Palestine cause know, is that the Arabs don't want any more Jews in Palestine.

When I finished *Roosevelt and Hopkins* all that I could think of was my Uncle Moe's comment about the 900 cattle, all of whom would have been saved.

VI. The Week After the Election of November 6, 2012

The week after the presidential election of November 6, 2012, PBS showed a four-hour documentary, *The Dust Bowl*. From 1934 until 1938 the entire middle of the country was transformed into one parched Sahara Desert, but without any oasis. There was no food, no water, no crops, no sunlight, no hope.

But as the documentary concludes, it shows newsreel clips of the President, in the back of his black convertible, wearing his familiar hat and waving, visiting the distressed farms and towns, driving through the dust bowl even though the wheels were almost bogged down in the sand. The President brings a message of hope, assuring the people that their government will do whatever was necessary to make their farms green again, and their lives happy and prosperous. And his deeds even exceeded his promises.

That one man, seemingly almost by his own fierce determination, had saved our country. By 1939, the year of the *St. Louis*, the green had begun to return, the first crocuses in five years. And the nation has prospered ever since.

It's been a long, private wrestling match, all in my mind. I know that it's over because I wish that I had been old enough to vote for him.

A CODA

I was editing my essays, hunting for an errant split-infinitive—none was found of course—when I began to wonder how many of those threads from the 1930s and 1940s were still in the weave, some 70 or 75 years later.

As I conjured up those hazy, distant days, my memories seemed to gather around one central theme—*kashrut.*

I recalled those endless discussions about food—was this or that dessert really *pareve*; was there any forbidden ingredient in a chocolate-covered Good Humor ice-cream pop; was rice kosher for Passover, and if so, what about Rice Krispies.

And about people—was this or that butcher trustworthy; was so-and-so, usually the lady upstairs in Apartment 4 C, really kosher; did this or that Jewish politician, one of those lads who could don and doff a yarlmulke in an instant, sometimes eat *treif* when he thought that no one was looking.

I could almost hear that endless chatter about food and people when *kashrut's* dominant element slowly emerged—space. Our Brooklyn apartment, on Ocean Avenue between Avenues I and J, had a small kitchen with small closets. The challenge, the mystery, was where to store our eight sets of dishes—two for *milchig* (one for every day and one for *Shabbos* and holidays), the same two sets for *fleishig*, then all sets multiplied by two for *Pesach*, plus the four sets of pots and pans, plus the (I forget how many) sets of flatware, silverware, tablecloths and napkins.

It was the contingent representing Passover that gave Mom pause because those items took up half the space but were so very sparingly used, especially since in those days we always had our Seders elsewhere. At one point Mom suggested that instead of having entire sets of everything just for the eight days of Passover, some prayer should be devised which would allow us to use our regular-season dishes instead; but that idea was rejected as too controversial, almost scandalous. Mom's response was that if the men had had to do all the work with the dishes that the women had to do, such a prayer would be devised in a minute.

Did I forget the drinking glasses? I don't remember how many sets we had, but I do remember that they were more fragile than the dishes and had to be handled and stored with particular care.

All that energy devoted to keeping kosher even though *kasrut* itself was on an elusive continuum that was hard to define. We thought of ourselves as being strictly kosher (see the discussion of dishes, *supra*), even though our synagogue, the East Midwood Jewish Center, was Conservative, not Orthodox. But many of our Orthodox neighbors would not eat in our home, even if we and they used the same butcher; and our neighbors more Orthodox still would not eat in *their* homes, *ad infinitum*. When I asked Dad about those immeasurable degrees of observance, he replied that we were kosher, but not fanatically so.

And now, some 70 or 75 years later, I'm even less fanatically so, and by a wide margin.

There is, in fact, only one rule of keeping kosher that I strictly observe: I do not knowingly eat any pork products—not just no ham, bacon, or sausages-- but no pork in any of its other and more hidden guises—no chorizo, pancetta, gammon, fuet, pepperoni, chitterlings, gelatin, cracklings, or porcine. Those masks may have fooled me early on, and that's why I say that I have never eaten any pork products knowingly.

The reason for that abstention goes back to the late summer of 1947, just as I was preparing to go off to college; Dad suddenly decided that I had to live off-campus in a kosher home, even, if need be, with a rabbi. I objected mightily, arguing that I did not intend to be kosher when I was an adult and on my own; to which the swift reply was that I was not there yet. Fortunately, Mom quickly interceded with one of her Henry Clay specials: I would be required to observe only one rule—I would not eat any pork products.

I accepted in an instant and have felt honor-bound to adhere to that family Missouri Compromise to this day, the compromise that steered me so safely and painlessly through my happy college years. It took just a few days during Freshman Orientation Week not to feel guilty about enjoying an ice-cream dessert after a veal parmigiana supper—but without the meat sauce, lest it contain even a trace of pork.

But dealing with shrimp, lobster, scallops and other forbidden seafoods has been a less abstemious, and perhaps less honorable, tale. I succumbed some time in the late '70s.

Our family (my wife, two young children and I) would often join others, not all of whom were Jewish, for an early Sunday dinner at a Chinese restaurant (Chin Chow Fu ?) on Broadway and the low 90s. Those theologically banned crustaceans would be included among the dishes ordered for the table, and as they were passed around, it wasn't possible or practical for me to limit my children to only the platters of vegetables, chicken, rice and tofu. Since I did not want to make a point of not eating what my own wife and children were eating, I indulged too.

Although by then time had tempered my guilt, I also had a back -up excuse: Mom had not mentioned any shellfish in her landmark settlement. But I also knew that my excuse was phony because the only reason for her omission was that words like *shrimp, lobster,* and *scallops* were probably not even in her vocabulary, whereas pork products were the very definition of foods that were *treif.* So I really knew, deep down, that I was violating the spirit of her compromise, which was not to eat anything that was blatantly non-kosher. But, of course, it was long after my college years.

Although I did begin to eat those prohibited—but tasty—sea creatures some 40 years ago, I still, to this day, do not allow them into my home, a rather partially-pregnant resolution. There may not be any logic to it, but it makes me feel comfortable. My Dad surely would have frowned in rejection, but Mom, who so often rescued me from my spasms of irreligious indiscretions, might have said that it was better than nothing.

All of which brings to mind the discussion back then explaining why we can't have a steak (medium rare) with a glass of milk (skim) in the first place. When I first asked that question, out of honest curiosity and not to be provocative, Dad answered by referring me to a passage from the Torah, from the Book of Exodus:

"Thou shalt not seethe a kid in its mother's milk." (23:19)

I remember it so clearly because I had not heard of the word *seethe*, and I looked it up immediately, but off to the side so as not to betray my ignorance; it means *to boil*, and that definition is still a bit arcane.

Lest I quibble about whether such a sentence would even a apply to a grilled hamburger with cheese, since neither boiling nor a goat would be involved, Dad immediately followed with a disquisition: Over the centuries the rabbis have expanded *seethe* to include *every* form of cooking—roasting, frying, broiling, sautéing, barbecuing, stewing, baking, currying, simmering, brazing, toasting, and any other style that cooks with heat; and at the same time, they also decided, in that same expansive sweep, that *kid* is a metaphor for *every* animal. He emphasized that those interpretations had been settled Jewish custom for centuries.

I saw an opportunity and filed a prompt objection: those interpretations and expansions were the distortions of Man, whereas Exodus was from Above. Said I: If the Author had wanted to include every cooking technique and every animal, He would have said so in plain Hebrew. I was in a Justice Scalia mode, arguing for the Untampered Original.

Taking a more poetic stance, Dad then asked if the concept of not cooking an animal in its mother's milk wasn't a beautiful one, and he was surprised, amazed really, that I agreed.

And as I think about it now, the idea is not only beautiful but spiritual, one of the few commandments against killing in the whole world that anybody actually observes. Not that I observe it myself.

Reflecting on my parents' many rules and regulations concerning *kashrut*, I sometimes wonder how my grandparents, long gone, would react to some of my irreligious ways.

My maternal grandparents, from distinguished families, emigrated from Vilna in the 1880s; my paternal forebears, from more humble backgrounds, came from Odessa or its surroundings in the 1890s. All were Orthodox, and all left what had been their family homes for generations in search of religious liberty, not only for themselves, but for their children, grandchildren, and all the generations beyond; they all had the same dream and fervent prayer—to be able to observe their Orthodoxy without fear or reservation. And America has been precisely such a wondrous place, a miracle that in their minds, and maybe even in my own, only God could have wrought.

And here am I, a beneficiary of their struggle and courage, eating a non-kosher hamburger with a glass of milk.

Would they be disappointed in me? I could argue, for the defense, that they emigrated for religious freedom, and who, I would note, personifies that better than I?

That raises the broadest of questions of whether any of it matters, a question that is not answerable, except perhaps by a lifetime of Torah immersion: Does being a Believer make one a better person? I'm far too ignorant to have an opinion, but even Maimonides and St. Thomas Aquinas struggled with it.

I remember when Dad announced, rather casually at a Friday night *Shabbos* meal, that one of our synagogue's most prestigious members, a Trustee, was not an honest man; at least one of Dad's friends had so confided. It was a statement that was memorable because it seemed to come out of nowhere, particularly since gossip was not my father's style. When I asked whether being observant made one a better person, a more ethical one, a more honest one, I was surprised when he said, "No".

Then why be observant?

Because it *teaches* you to be honest, but it can't *make* you be honest. When I followed by inquiring whether observant people were more *likely* to be honest than the unobservant, I was stunned by his forthrightness when he said that he doubted that, that his experience told him that there was no correlation. I should leave it there, because the further explanation was too murky for me—that being observant and being religious were not the same, that truly religious people were honest, but that did not make them more honest than those who were irreligious.

But hold on; I'm getting wildly egocentric because my grandparents have many descendants, and they represent a wide swath of religious devotion from the almost Orthodox to those completely indifferent. I'm somewhere in the vague, mushy middle.

I belong to a synagogue, albeit a Reform one, no *yalmulke* required although I usually wear one for old time's sake; I attend services on the High Holy Days, but only very occasionally during the year; I observe Chanukah by lighting candles on each of the eight days, but I never chant more than a few lines from *Mor-Otzur* and it never takes more than three or four by-rote minutes; and I have a *mezuzah* on my doorpost, but I still haven't replaced the passages from Scriptures (Deuteronomy 6:4; 11:13) which fell out long ago.

The weave from the 1930s and 1940s may still be vaguely visible, but I must acknowledge that it is now quite threadbare.

ABOUT THE AUTHOR

Mordecai Rosenfeld was born in Brooklyn in 1930. He attended the local public schools (P.S. 152; Midwood H.S.) and is a graduate of Brown (A.B. 1951) and Yale Law School (LL.B. 1954).

He spent almost his entire legal career as a solo practitioner in New York, representing small investors who challenged corporate and financial greed. He won some and lost some and retired from the law in 1993.

For some twenty-two years he wrote a monthly column for *The New York Law Journal*, and those essays were collected and published in two books: *The Lament of the Single Practitioner* (Univ. Georgia Press, 1988) and *A Backhanded View of the Law—Irreverent Essays on Justice* (Ox Bow Press, 1992). Louis Auchincloss wrote the Foreword for each ("these essays [drown] pomposity and bureaucracy and even man's inhumanity to man in waves of devastating laughter"). Both collections received rave reviews from the *Times Literary Supplement* (*TLS*) (London): "beautifully adept jabs at legal idiocies, Swiftian". Dee Brown (*Bury My Heart at Wounded Knee*) wrote, "his style is remindful of the declarative mode of Addison and Steele, with sometimes the charm of Dean Swift. No matter the mood in which it may be written, any Rosenfeld essay is a tonic that can restore the spirits." One of his essays is included in *The Norton Reader* (10th Ed.).

Rosenfeld received the Bruce K. Gould Award for a distinguished book on the law.

His essays on poetry have appeared in *PN Review*, a British literary magazine.

Rosenfeld published two essays in *Poetica Magazine* (on line) in 2012, and both appear in this collection.

He is a member of PEN, and lives with his wife in Greenwich Village.